YOU CAN BE A SUPER AUTHOR TOO!
15 Ordinary People Writing
Life Changing Amazing Stories

Compiled by Bestselling Author
Sharon C. Jenkins

Copyright ©2022 by Sharon C. Jenkins

All rights reserved. This book or any portion thereof may not be reproduced or used in any manner whatsoever without the express written permission of the publisher except for the use of brief quotations in a book review.

Printed in the United States of America
ISBN: 978-1-7337907-2-7

Published by Sunshine Reigns Publishing Company a Subsidiary of The Master Communicator's Writing Services

www.mcwritingservices.com

TABLE OF CONTENTS

5   Dedication

7   Who is Sharon C. Jenkins?

9   Experienced Super Authors Introduction

15   Nuggets of Wisdom from Experienced Super Authors Still Wearing Their Cape Proudly…

17   Super Authors

95   Closing Thoughts

97   About the Compiler

DEDICATION

Super Authors rule the literary world! It's time to celebrate them for their bravery. This book is for YOU!

Your personal journey is unique. You might write primarily for money, or because writing is in your DNA.

WHO IS SHARON C. JENKINS?

Over fifty years of literary expression stands behind me. I started writing at age eight—a time when children were not allowed to speak. In defiance, I penned poetry to release my ideas into the world. My self-discovery flourished from that point. As a teenager in the late 1960's, my poems took on the voice of the civil rights revolution. I fell madly in love with the likes of Maya Angelo, Nikki Giovanni, and "The Last Poets." Then I laid down my pen as a young mother. Marriage and raising children consumed my time. Divorce returned me to that old, dependable friend: the pen. I finally discovered my writing voice in the late 1980's.

A big, mean woman inspired and challenged me. At least that's how I perceived her. She invited me to read poetry in a group at her home. I was thinking Greenwich Village, sitting in a dark, sultry place, listening to jazz, and snapping our fingers after every piece. I imagined vivid scenes. Then, if the world didn't play out the way I wanted it to, I could revert to my imagined happy place. The woman wanted us to perform spoken word poetry. She offended my introvert pride when she criticized my rhythm and diction. Discontent was written across my face. The "mean" woman angered me.

Later, a much different—young, nice—lady named Lorna invited me to a drama class. I lacked courage to go along with things of this nature, but my anger substituted for courage. It motivated me to do the unthinkable: go to drama class. I spent a telephone call to Lorna, complaining about the "mean" woman. I also explained that I was "just going to watch" and would "make my decision later" about joining the class. She assured me that I could do just that. When I entered through the door, I found my scared self a seat. Lorna was late. I prepared to watch the class from the back of the room.

A large, grandmother-like woman walked on stage to prepare us for the class. Mrs. Parks took one look at me and called me to the front. I politely told her that I was there to watch. She politely told me, "No one comes into my class and does not participate." It was a divine set-up. I was taught to respect my elders. Being the liberated woman I was, it was a struggle to do so, but I did. One year later, I performed the "mean" woman's poetry. I spoke my poems wherever they were welcomed. This brings us to the business of writing…

Your personal journey is unique. You might write primarily for money, or because writing is in your DNA. Perhaps your passion for your message will not let you walk away from the blank page. I am a member of the "book-ish" tribe. People in my clan often got lost in the passion of writing, ignoring the practical business elements. What stands in the gap between passionate writer and published author? YOU! You are a super author in the making!

One bit of advice: Don't run away from "big mean women", run to them. It may be a challenge that revolutionizes your life. For some of you, conquering the business side of writing is that challenge.

Happy Writing!!!

EXPERIENCED SUPER AUTHORS INTRODUCTION

The premiere book in the Super Author Series is titled Are You a Super Author? I invited three of the authors in that edition to share their wisdom in this book. The focus in this book is on showcasing everyday people with an extraordinary vision to write their hearts out. These generals have successfully balanced their career and their desire to write and done it well. Ladies and gentlemen I would like to introduce to you, Melanie Bragg, Sharon Norris Elliott, Brian W. Smith, and Matilda Butler.

MELANIE BRAGG

Melanie Bragg is the owner of Bragg Law, a general civil firm in Houston, Texas. She is the author of three books: *Crosstown Park*, an Alex Stockton legal thriller, published by Koehler Books; *Defining Moments: Insights into the Lawyer's Soul*, an American Bar Association Flagship publication and *HIPPA for the General Practitioner*, also published by the American Bar Association. She is a former Chair of the American Bar Association Solo, Small Firm & General Practice Division and is currently a Delegate to the ABA House of Delegates. She is in her third year as a trustee on the Texas Bar Foundation Board of Trustees and was recently appointed to a 3-year term on the State Bar of Texas TLAP committee. Bragg writes on mindfulness and leadership with her monthly columns for the GP Solo eReport and teaches the same in her workshops. She is a certified Success Coach. Please contact me at Melanie@melaniebragg.com or https://www.melaniebragg.com) for comments or feedback.

SHARON NORRIS ELLIOTT

"Live significantly!" That's the inspiring message of Sharon Norris Elliott, award-winning author, popular speaker, astute Bible teacher, and founder/CEO of *Life That Matters Ministries and AuthorizeMe®*. She encourages everyone who will listen to live a life that matters. Some of her 12 published titles include:
- *A Woman God Can Bless*
- *366 Glimpses of God: Getting to Know the God Who Knows You*
- *Why I Get into Trouble* (the first title of her 7-book children's series);
- *Boomerangs to Arrows: A Godly Guide for Launching Young Adult Children*; and
- *Power Suit: the Armor of God Fit for the Feminine Frame.*
  Two new projects are on the horizon for early 2022
- *Didn't See That Coming: When How They're Living's Not How You Raised Them*
- *I Really Need to Know Children's Series* (This 7-book series is theology for little kids and will cover topics our 3 to 7-year-olds can understand: the sin nature, death, the Trinity, baptism, communion, forgiveness, and greed.

Discover more books and her devotional blog at her ministry website, www.LifeThatMatters.net.

Sharon is amazed at how God's goodness has brought her from being "Straight Outta Compton" to standing before great people and audiences. Dedicated to teaching and learning, she is a cum laude college graduate (Biola University), recipient of an honorary Doctor of Divinity Degree, and member of several prestigious organizations (ACE, AWSA, SCBWI). Sharon is also a religious broadcaster hosting her own show, Life That Matters with Sharon Norris Elliott, on The Holy Spirit Broadcasting Network (HSBN.tv), and the Christian Women's Word Network (CWWN.tv). The show is also available on Facebook Live, Spotify and several other platforms. Her new podcast, *Sixty-sational*, is also in the works.

Under the *Life That Matters Ministries* umbrella, are her two companies. *Milk & Honey Life Retreats* rival any other girls' getaway for both fun and faith enhancement. Through her *AuthorizeMe® Consulting, Coaching, & Editing Firm, and Literary Agency LLC*. Sharon edits others' work, mentors up-and-coming writers and speakers, coaches writers as they draft their manuscripts, and conducts hands-on seminars personally assisting attendees toward their publishing goals. The latest exciting growth of her AuthorizeMe® brand includes her new move to function as a literary agent.

Sharon is retired from her esteemed 35-year teaching career and now focuses full time on her writing, editing, agenting, and broadcasting. She and her husband James serve at Christ Second Baptist Church in Long Beach, CA, where Sharon is an assistant minister. They enjoy their empty nest, traveling, and visiting their children and grandchildren.

BRIAN W. SMITH

Brian W. Smith is the award winning, bestselling author of thirty-seven novels and screenplays. His novels have appeared on numerous bestsellers list: Dallas Morning News, Amazon, Target Retail Stores, and others. He has also ghost written 20 novel, memoirs, and non-fiction books for other authors. He has also been signed to Simon and Schuster since 2011.

Brian is the Founder/President of *The Script Repository* (a company that specializes in adapting novels to screenplays).

When Brian is not writing novels and screenplays for himself and others, he has served as an Adjunct Professor of Creative Writing and Screenwriting at Collin College (Plano, TX) since 2012.

Brian's educational background includes:
- Master of Business Administration (MBA)
- Bachelor of Science in Business Administration
- Bachelor of Science in Social Science

Brian is a native of New Orleans, La., and currently resides in McKinney, TX.

MATILDA BUTLER

Writing Alchemy: *How to Write Fast and Deep*, four anthologies of award-winning stories entitled *Seasons of Our Lives: Spring, Summer, Autumn, Winter, and the collective memoir Rosie's Daughters: The "First Woman To" Generation Tells Its Story* all draw on Matilda Butler's 50 years of research training and work experiences. In addition to being an award-winning author, she is a social psychologist, authorpreneur, conference presenter, and memoir coach with a passion for helping others tell their stories in powerful and engaging ways.

Matilda taught and conducted research at Stanford University, created the nationwide Women's Educational Equity Communication Network, and co-founded Knowledge Access International, a software company specializing in CD-ROM information products. After selling the company in 1997, she returned to research and writing that initially resulted in *Rosie's Daughters*, the story of the generation of women born during WWII, shaped by the 60s, who didn't take "no" for an answer.

Her more than 100 interviews for the collective memoir showed her the value and importance of telling life stories. With that insight, she began teaching memoir writing classes and started the website: www.WomensMemoirs.com After several years of teaching, she felt there had to be a better way to help students become purposeful writers. She and her co-author Kendra Bonnett developed a new system for writing they call Writing Alchemy.

Prior to her work in the field of memoir, Matilda published more than 100 professional articles, contributed chapters to published books about women in education and work, co-authored the award-winning book *Women and the Mass Media* and co-edited the book *Knowledge Utilization Systems*.

She graduated magna cum laude from Boston University, received her M.A. in communication research from Stanford University and her Ph.D. in social psychology from Northwestern University. She has been listed in *Who's Who in the West* since 1978 and *Who's Who of American Women* since 1975.

Like the women in *Rosie's Daughters*, Matilda is a member of the "First Woman To" Generation and also had to find her way in a world turned upside down by the social, cultural and historic changes of the past 50+ years. She moved to Oregon four years ago and currently splits her time between Corvallis and Waikoloa Beach.

NUGGETS OF WISDOM FROM EXPERIENCED SUPER AUTHORS STILL WEARING THEIR CAPE PROUDLY…

BEING AN
AUTHOR
IS A LOT
OF WORK.

MAXIMIZE YOUR AUTHOR EXPERIENCE

By Melanie Bragg

The road to becoming an author can start early, like it did for me in second grade when I typed the *Story of my Life* in red ink on my Mother's typewriter, or it can start much later. But one thing is for certain-being an author in today's times is much more than typing away at your desk and then sending the manuscript by snail-mail to a publisher with an in-house editor who will correct all of your typos, then print and market it for you. For an author to sit back and receive big fat royalty checks is a thing of the past and I am not sure it ever existed. The bottom line is: BEING AN AUTHOR IS A LOT OF WORK. You have to really love it and do everything you need to do in order to be successful. And, the writing part of being an author is just the beginning.

The word *authorpreneur* encompasses the skills required to be an author in today's world. Writers come in all shapes and sizes. They find time to write on the bus, the train, before work, in between shifts- whatever it takes to get the job done. It is the *love* of writing that keeps them going.

In recent years the publishing world has undergone a radical transformation. The industry is still in transition. Agents and traditional publishers are changing the way they do things. Anyone with the tenacity to actually sit down and write their manuscript AND ample funds in their pocketbook can get published. The big publishing houses are keeping up with the times by opening their own self-publishing branches.

Authors have different motivations for getting published. Some just want to tell their stories or get their message across: Vanity Press. Or they want to tell someone else's story: True Crime. Biography. Others want to be the female John Grisham: Melanie Bragg. Some think they have written or will write the "great American novel." The truth is that most everyone has a book in them and if you are a writer you have probably been approached by folks with a "great idea" for a book they want YOU to write for them. I tell them to learn the "craft" of writing and dig in. Most writers I know already have their stories in mind and are busy working to accomplish their own goals.

There is a wealth of information on the market today about the *craft* of writing. In his book *On Writing*, Steven King gives a great overview of the process. I was lucky to have the late, great Rita Gallagher, co-founder of RWA (Romance Writers of America,) teach me the craft of fiction writing and novel structure. The education was priceless. I remember fondly the four years of spending all day every Friday soaking up her wisdom. She will always be my writing angel and the picture of her inward and outward beauty is in my mind's eye when I write. I can hear her say, "Every word is a dollar to an editor" to teach me that less is best.

HERE IS THE GOOD NEWS: Sugar coating the hard work involved doesn't help anyone. But there is no doubt that accomplishing your life-long dream of publishing a book and being satisfied with the quality of the book is what I call the "elixir of accomplishing your true purpose in life."

For me, someone who was born to write, all of the effort is worth it and I would not trade it for anything in the world. I want to share my lessons learned so that you will be better prepared to have success in your writing career.

So here we go for the "best practices" I want you to know NOW:
1) Writers must learn to listen to others but to always follow their own gut: People are well meaning most of the time, but sometimes they just plain don't know what they are talking about. It is kind of like asking your spouse to edit your book- boy is that ever a set up. Of course they are going to love it. An impartial, disinterested person should always be your editor.

But what I mean here is that you should always know that your judgment as an author is best. It is good to get information from books, teachers and critique groups but in the final analysis if you feel strongly about something in your manuscript, you should go with it. I learned this from my critique group. Everything I debated with my teacher to keep in would be the very thing every month that the class loved. It taught me to take the teacher's advice or the student's feedback, but to keep the things I felt very strongly about because they would resonate with audiences.

An example of this was the beginning of my first fiction novel, *Crosstown Park*. Everything you read about starting a novel says that you have to start with a big impact, a big crisis so my first draft started with a courtroom scene. It never resonated with me and I felt very strongly the story starts when Alex meets the Reverend. It was the most important part of the story, even though it was not a big climax or catastrophe, because it was the beginning of a major shift in the main character's life. Sometimes those events can be subtle and seem small but in retrospect they are life-changing. In the final version, I went with my gut to keep it at the plane scene and was so pleased when so many readers commented that they loved how the story began. Two points for me following my own best judgment. Do the same in your work and you will be happy and turn out a better final product.

2) Writers must develop a marketing plan-with their a) vision, b) framework, and c) the build-out phase:

I teach a class on this but let me say that you have to start with your VISION.

How do you see yourself and the book once it is done?
What are your goals for the book?
Do you want to keep writing after this project?
Do you know the reality of how much it costs; how much time it takes?
How long it takes to get the pay off? What is the pay off?
Have you really researched the business?
Are you realistic about your vision and your goals?

Taking a deep breath and giving it some deep thought here will go a long way.

Many people think writing is easy until they try. They think that making an A on a paper in high school English makes them a writer. I actually thought that. Rita used to look up at me when I was impatient during class and say, "How long did it take you to be a lawyer?" I would say, "Four years of college and three years of law school." She would say, "Did you really think you could be a writer with no effort?" I would always shrug my shoulders and give her a sheepish grin and say, "Yes." After awhile I got the message that the "sweat equity" in writing is the same as anything else in life. You have to be your own Rocky and JUST DO IT!

The FRAMEWORK is what you do to learn the craft, what writing groups you join, what events you attend, and what you learn about the business of writing. Planning in advance, knowing who your market is, making sure you have non-fiction hooks in your fiction so you have lots of things to talk to audiences about is crucial in this phase.

The BUILD OUT is the fun part after publication. If you have done the vision and the framework well, then you will have fun. During the build out you are speaking and doing events all the time and really getting the word out on your book. You cannot wait and plan everything after the book comes out. It is an organic process and as much as you plan, other things happen. It is truly a delightful experience and one you want to enjoy. I did twenty-one (21) events in ninety (90) days after my fiction book came out and I learned an incredible amount about being an author in a very short period of time. I had to muster all of the strength and confidence I had and then enjoyed the ride.

After all, I spent many years creatively visualizing the day when I would be the author in a Barnes & Noble store. I can honestly say the reality is every bit as good as the dream and when I am doing a book event I feel as authentic as I can be. I am the person I was born to be.

With this first book, *Crosstown Park*, I spent the time establishing relationships with the store CRM's- the community relations managers- so that when *All One Blood*, the sequel, comes out I will be welcomed back with open arms. One word about the bookstores: I focused on selling my books but more than that I focused on giving the customers in the store a good experience with me, the author. That is what the stores like. They want to be seen in the community as supporting authors and providing interesting authors in the store. Remember, it is a marathon, not a jog.

One CRM told me a story about how Deepak Chopra stayed at a book signing until 1:00 AM, until the last person was taken care of, and when the CRM thanked him he said, "It is my honor. I still remember the days when I came in and sat at a table and no one even stopped to talk to me." I loved that the CRM shared that story with me because it made me feel like he understood that all authors start somewhere. If Deepak Chopra went through what I am going through then it is all right. You just have to keep going-get up on the horse and stay in the saddle.

3) Writers must become interested in and support other writers.

Become an activist- get involved in books. Join your local writing groups, get in a critique group, read magazines, sign up for blogs, look outside your genre. It is important to learn the craft and to know what is going on out there. Build your platform and your following. Make sure the people you meet are added to your list. Ask them, "May I put you on a list to receive notices of my book signings?" Write a blog. Send out newsletters. Promote other authors. When people see you promoting other authors you become the go-to guy or girl in the business. People want to hear from you because you are in the know. This is your world, be a leader.

Some authors just live in a vacuum and only think of their book. But the really successful ones I know are active. They support other authors online and in social marketing groups. It is kind of a "scratch my back" and "I'll scratch yours" world, so the more you spread the word about others who may be ahead of you, the more people you will have behind you in terms of spreading the word about yours. If you are an island, it will be very lonely when the book comes out and does not sell.

Surround yourself with people who want what you want and help them get where they are going and you will get farther. You don't have to get it back directly from those you give to and if you think you will, you will be disappointed. Think of it as sowing lots of seeds so that there will be a harvest for you when the time comes.

4) Writers must develop multimedia skills and social marketing skills: You must have a strong online presence with Facebook, LinkedIn, Google+, Goodreads, Amazon, Instagram, Pinterest and any other site

relevant to your market.

If you are saying to yourself that you don't like Facebook- STOP IT! Facebook is an invaluable tool. And I promise, I do not spend that much time on Facebook. I have managed to integrate it into my life as a pleasurable activity that does not take long. It is paying out big dividends. Social marketing does not always work instantly and you do not always get instant feedback on it, but plug ahead anyway. And like I said in number 3 above, keep giving. You "like" people's stuff, you comment on their threads and they will come to you and their friends will come to you. Take courses that make it easier for you and learn simple things all the time.

One example I can give you is one day I walked into court and several people asked me about Crosstown Park. They had seen it on Facebook. The word had spread with little effort on my part other than to post photos of my book events. I had reached what felt like a celebrity status and didn't even know it. People are watching whether they comment or not. They respect you for following through on your dream.

The value of social marketing is not always apparent, but don't let that stop you! Develop a practice of spending a little time in the morning and a little time in the evening on it and it will multiply.

Don't over-post. Let your public miss you and wonder what exciting things you have been doing while you have been offline. You can create a lot of buzz that way. The mystery of you...

5) Writers must be their own publicist (or hire one at several thousand dollars a pop):
If you have a big budget you can hire a publicist but make sure and research them thoroughly, make sure you know what they are going to do for you, talk to some of their other clients, and be fully aware going in what your duties are and what their duties are. I have not heard a lot of great publicist stories and since I am such a natural self-promoter, I have not met the right person for the right price to promote me-yet.

You are the best person to promote you. Mind your blog, promote your book, and do everything you can to have the most visibility.

6) Writers must become public speakers:
To be a successful author it is imperative you can speak in front of a group and give a good talk. After Crosstown Park came out, doing twenty-one (21) events in ninety (90) days taught me real fast that you need to have a plan and you need to follow that plan and then leave room for what happens in the group dynamic.

The place to start getting time in front of an audience is one of your many local Toastmasters groups. When you get a little more polished, I would suggest the National Speakers Association chapter in your locale. I qualified to become a Professional Speaker with the national organization, the National Speakers Association and got on the Board of my local chapter, NSA Houston, and that put me in touch with the monthly speakers. I get invited to the speaker dinners and lunches so my skills as a speaker are growing due to my involvement. Plus I get to fellowship with like-minded folks. There are lots of coaches and each meeting is a workshop on a different aspect of public speaking teaching us skills all authors need to know about, like story-telling. These skills will come in handy at your author events. Plus it helps you build your "list."

There are many different forms of author events. There are pre-launch parties, launch parties, book signings, book events, book panels, book fairs, book festivals, book conferences, book clubs to name a few. What you talk about is different for each one and you have to use a different set of skills. Some of it you talk to a group, some of it you talk to individuals, but you have to learn how to talk about your book in the best way. You have to enroll people into wanting to read the book. It can be a challenge to talk about yourself and your book all the time. Even for the outgoing types like myself.

At the events you have to be able to talk to and respond to a variety of people, all the while fielding questions about the book. The most frequently asked question is, "How long did it take to write?" You want to create a compelling story around this inevitable question. There are many paths to choose here and I confess I did mine by trial and error until I came up with what feels comfortable to me. Don't think you have to come up with something new each time. Think about how little kids like to hear the same story over and over. Audiences are the same. Hone your stories and tell them time and time again.

The audience will think of things you never thought of when you wrote the book. And you have to be prepared to respond to mistakes. For instance, an old high school friend of mine showed up at a book signing and I was so excited. Then he told me, "You called the thing in the middle of the road a medium instead of a median." He thought it was a typographical error. In fact, it was intentional and my editor did not catch it. Note to self: editors are humans too.

I always thought the middle of the road was the medium! What an enlightened moment I had when I learned for the first time that it was a median, not a medium. I tend to do that with words sometimes and it doesn't even bother me. It shows how closely people eye your work. Instead of being upset about the mistake, I enjoyed it and the crowd appreciated that I did not defend it or try to explain it away. Audiences love us when we are human. The more vulnerable you are, the more fun you will have.

The audience also wants to know how you came up with the idea for the story and a little bit about the background of the story. I have tried out many different aspects of the process with a variety of groups and it depends upon your audience. That is where practice comes in handy, especially when you can rehearse in front of a supportive and impartial group before you get to the real audiences.

Next time, I will be more prepared because I learned much of this when Crosstown Park was released a month early- yes I went into a panic mode when it was released a month early. I was happy to be as prepared as I was. My goal is for you to be prepared. I want you to be the best you can be.

7) Writers must take a deep breath, place hand over heart, repeat. Yes-because after book one is book two. The whole process begins again. And eventually, like saving money in the bank, the work you have done begins to multiply for you. You become an established author with an audience who loves to read your books.

Does it sound tough or overwhelming? I hope you are motivated and encouraged that despite how much work it is, being a successful published author is the elixir of life, a secret potion to your enhance your long-term happiness and fulfillment. Armchair writers or Monday morning quarterbacks will not advance your career. In fact they can kill your dream real fast. Power through it, make a plan, stick to your plan, and follow my motto: Never, Ever Give Up! and you will do fine.

ONCE I STARTED WRITING, I LEARNED THAT WRITING AND SPEAKING GO HAND IN HAND...

MY CALL TO MINISTRY

By Dr. Sharon Norris Elliott, ThD

My call to the speaking and preaching ministry grew out of doors opening. In my late teens and early twenties, I was a member of a professional gospel group, The Voices of Joi (Joi stood for "Jesus our Inspiration). We would introduce our songs with testimonies or words of challenge or encouragement. We would also give an invitation at the end of our concerts and encourage people to join a 4-week introduction to the faith course. I taught the women who enrolled. Then we'd get those people plugged into a local church. I transferred from USC to Biola University to be able to seriously study the Bible in an academic context.

Other than one semester of changing my major to Religion while I was at USC, I had no thoughts at this point about going into ministry of any kind. I was studying to be a schoolteacher. While I was a student at Biola, I visited a church where my father was executive pastor. That congregation would ask visitors to stand and give a hello statement. I don't know what I said, but my daddy stood up, walked to the front edge of the pulpit area, pointed to me, and said, "There's the preacher!" It was as if he had been praying and waiting to see which one of his three kids would step into his calling. The neat thing is that all three of us serve in ministry now; Daddy just happened to hear something in me that day and he made sure to point it out.

Once I started writing, I learned that writing and speaking go hand in hand, so I joined an organization that taught Christian speakers to speak (CLASS = Christian Leaders, Authors, and Speakers Services). I then became a teaching staff member with CLASS. I also taught in Christian schools where I was able to teach the Word every day in class, regularly in chapel services, and in the religion courses specifically. I started receiving invitations to speak and preach and people confirmed my gift with their comments about hearing God speak to them through my messages.

All the while, I was also in leadership at my church teaching Sunday school, leading and teaching in the women's ministry, and sometimes preaching. My pastor conferred on me a ministry license so I can marry 'em and bury 'em.

I attended seminary for a short while but ran out of money to pay that tuition. Then a school of ministry ordained me in the office of Prophetess and conferred upon me an honorary Doctor of Divinity (DDiv). That has since been upgraded to a full Doctor of Theology (ThD, thanks in part to my 12 books being accepted as my thesis) when that school of ministry became an affiliate with the seminary I had been attending. Couple all of that with my sheer love of teaching the Word and my life and experiences have come together for me to understand my call to preach through both the vocal and written word.

Here are some lessons that I have learned along the way:

- Be teachable - Stick with but expand upon the initial vision God gave you about your writing. Others in the business have been moved by God to be in positions to assist you and help grow the seeds you've been given.

- Be excellent - Strive to do everything with excellence. Learn your craft. Writers can spell, they understand syntax, they show rather than tell, etc. And keep your business life in excellent order - meet deadlines, keep appointments, keep up and be honest with business expenses, keep precise records, pay your taxes, etc.

- Stay alert - Opportunities will always present themselves. Discern between an opportunity and a greedy grab. Go only through the doors that God opens.

- BONUS TIP - Never be afraid to help another author. You know the command: Do unto others as you would have them do unto you.

AUTHORPRENEURSHIP, THE BASTARD LOVE CHILD OF TWO WORDS (AUTHOR AND ENTREPRENEURSHIP) THAT WERE ONCE TABOO TO MENTION IN THE SAME SENTENCE.

AUTHORPRENEURSHIP, I DID IT MY WAY

By Brian W. Smith

Authorpreneurship, the bastard love child of two words (author and entrepreneurship) that were once taboo to mention in the same sentence. A mythical word that was more elusive than *Bigfoot* or the *Loch Ness Monster*. A word that once moved *real* writers (those scribes who spout Shakespeare while pecking away on antique typewriters) to deem anyone audacious enough to utter the word, a low-life cheater of the writing craft who deserved to perish under a pile of publishing house rejection letters.

Oh, but how times have changed. Fortunately for me, the change started to take place shortly after I entered this literary industry in 2006—the same year a Harvard student named Zuckerberg took his social media company, Facebook, from being a restricted site and opened it up to anyone thirteen years and older with an email address.

I was a freshly minted MBA, who was naïve to the way things were done in the fickle world of publishing. My background was in business. I flaunted a corporate title; took advantage of a corporate expense account; and viewed all things business through a pair of corporate lenses. All decision making started with a SWOT Analysis and ended with a clearly defined ROI. It was a way of thinking that helped me climb the corporate ladder and I was sure it would serve me well in the publishing industry.

Prior to penning my first manuscript, I'd never written any fiction. In fact, I could count on one hand the number of fiction books I'd ever read. My leisurely reading was reserved for books that talked about ways to earn more money, get the next promotion, and how to inspire and motivate people. Even after I released my first novel and opened my publishing company (Hollygrove Publishing), I often told anyone who asked, "I'm not a writer who owns a business. I'm a businessman who happens to write." Every time I spouted that line, real writers would glare at me like they wanted to stab my eyes with their dull, eraser-less, pencils.

Fast forward nearly ten years. Book stores in the United States have been closing faster than authors can trade their desktop computers in for laptops. Physical book sales (hardcover and paperback) have plummeted. More and more readers walk around with their entire inventory of books in their purses—stored safely on an electronic device that's smaller than a standard size spiral notepad. The literary industry has taken a stroll down electronic lane, and it ain't coming back—and I for one, am glad.

Why am I glad? I'll tell you. I'm glad the literary industry has become more electronic because my skill set and *authorpreneurship* mentality (that used to make my peers give me the side-eye and brand me a faker), is no longer viewed as a curse. In fact, my background has been the primary reason I've been able to survive in this high stress—low profit industry.

Some authors I encounter, the ones who despise the business side of the job, hope and pray that the industry goes back to the days of five and six figure advances, publisher sponsored book tours for mid-list authors, and royalty checks that sponsored summer family vacations. I just listen to their ramblings; shaking my head pitifully. Sometimes I feel like I'm listening to a forty year old, former high school football star, going on and on about the good old days. Their eyes glaze over. Smirks creep onto their faces. Their pleasant memories can be viewed on their foreheads. I allow them their moments. Watching them bask in the past is both entertaining and sad. I don't have the heart to tell them that things are never going to go back to the way they used to be.

The truth of the matter is, no one knows for sure that things are going to go back to the way they used to be. After all, the cassette tape made a comeback…oops, no it didn't. The VHS recorder still holds a lot of value… my bad, that's another bad example. All jokes aside, despite all of the examples around us that once technology gets its foot into an industry there is no turning back, many authors still believe that the hardcover novel is going to make a comeback, publishers are going to start once again writing huge checks, and the need for authors to transform into *authorpreneurs* is going to fade away.

I for one don't believe things will change and I have two personal experiences to back up my claim: my experience once I signed a deal with Strebor/Simon and Schuster and my job as an Adjunct Professor.

In 2012, I signed a one book deal with Strebor/Simon and Schuster. After spending my first six years as a self-published author, it was refreshing to allow someone else take on the grunt work of producing, distributing, and promoting my novel. But a funny thing happened after I cashed my advance check—life as an author signed to a "major" wasn't, as the kids say, *all that*. Yeah, it was cool walking into a few major retail outlets and seeing my book on the shelves, but after the excitement died and it was time to get down to the business of selling books, life as a traditionally published author seemed a lot like my life as a self-published author. Marketing my book was my responsibility. Coordinating my book signings was my responsibility. Scheduling interviews on radio shows was my responsibility. Trying to figure out ways to get more readers to buy the book before retailers packaged them up in ninety days and shipped them back to the publisher—thus ruining my chance of receiving any royalty check—was ultimately my responsibility. I enjoyed the prestige that came with being able to say I had a major book deal, but it was my experiences in the world of *authorpreneurship* that enabled me to survive that not so pleasant time.

During the latter part of 2012, I accepted an Adjunct Professor position in the Creative Writing Division of a community college. Imagine my surprise when I wasn't asked to teach the traditional Creative Writing type classes: *How to Write a Strong Antagonist* or *How to Write in Third Person*. The department coordinator asked me to teach several *authorpreneurship* style classes. Classes with titles like: *How to Market and Promote Your Novel and How to Self-Publish Your Novel*.

When I got the news that I'd been hired to teach those *authorpreneurship* style classes I wanted to go on one of the Social Media "Author Groups" I'm a member of, and rub the news of my new teaching *gig* in the face of all of those *real* authors who once swore that entertaining thoughts of the business side of writing guaranteed all struggling authors a one-way trip to literary purgatory. I didn't gloat, but I did get a picture of one of my classes—filled with nearly thirty aspiring authors eager to learn the ways of the *authorpreneur*.

As I survey the literary landscape these days, I've noticed two things: many real authors who refused to get off high-horses and become *authorpreneurs* have lost their book deals and eBooks are sending physical books the way of the dinosaur. Authors who understand the importance of establishing multiple promotional platforms, hone their communication skills, and identify multiple sales vehicles—all key components of an *authorpreneurs* arsenal—will be the people who survive the ebb and flows of this volatile industry.

TELLING PERSONAL
STORIES IS A VALUABLE
FORM OF HEALING
FOR MANY WRITERS
AND STORYTELLERS.

YOU CAN BE AN AUTHORPRENEUR... REALLY

By Matilda Butler

What? I know you may still be working on writing your book, but now you realize you need to be an authorpreneur. It can sound overwhelming, so let's start with the fun part.

Imagine this.

It's May 30, a warm, sunny, late afternoon in Los Angeles. You arrive at the Miyako Hotel, unpack, put on your finery, comb your hair, add red lipstick and a touch of blush, and catch a cab to the Wells Fargo Building. The elevator takes you to the fifty-fourth floor, where you see that the lights of the city are beginning to twinkle through the large window panels as the sun sets. The reason for your visit? You're receiving a national book award, an IPPY.

You know why you're there, but still you have an unexpected and more-than-ample supply of butterflies in your stomach and your hands are a little sweaty. Then the thrill when the emcee announces in a booming voice, "And the winner is…" Suddenly you are at the front of the room, not sure how you managed to walk up there. Everyone is clapping. The emcee puts the medal around your neck and shakes your damp hand. You even manage to hold your book so that the cover shows clearly. Photographs capture the moment.

IT'S ALL PART OF BEING AN AUTHORPRENEUR

Are you amazed this happened? Do you say, "I can't believe this?" Or perhaps "I don't deserve this?" No. Getting a book award doesn't just happen. The world doesn't decide to clap for all your hard work on its own. Readers, or potential readers, don't line up to purchase your book mysteriously. I like the way Sharon Jenkins addresses this point in her book *Authorpreneurship: The Business Start-Up Manual for Authors.* She has an entire chapter entitled, "If I Write It, They Will Come…Or Not." Writing success requires a plan you put into place, your plan as an authorpreneur.

And yes, that's me receiving an IPPY (and eventually three other book awards) for my collective memoir, *Rosie's Daughters: The "First Woman To" Generation Tells Its Story.* I had even practiced how to hold the book so that the cover would show up in photographs. Small details that lead to success take planning and effort. The mindset is still the same: you are determining and handling your writing career—your way.

BECOMING AN AUTHORPRENEUR: MY STORY

This part of the tale begins with *Rosie's Daughters*, a collective memoir of American women born during World War II, precursors of the Baby Boom generation.

Rosie the Riveter is a mythic figure in our culture, with good reason—she built ships, flew bombers, and filled thousands of other essential wartime jobs, upending traditional views of "women's work." When the war was over, however, American industry thanked Rosie and merely sent her home. Rosie's "daughters," however, grew up and flung wide the doors of employment opportunity that Rosie had unlocked. These women can claim more career "firsts" and greater sociocultural change than any other generation.

I'm a "Rosie's daughter," and my tale began after attending the fortieth reunion of my high school class. In one session, we were seated around tables in the cavernous room where four decades earlier I had studied English Lit, American History, French, and Algebra every afternoon and evening. Representatives of each quinquennial reunion class spoke about their experiences, telling stories that were alternatively humorous and serious because of the momentous times in which we all have lived. I was struck by how the stories of my class differed from those of women who graduated even five years earlier or later.

Once back in my California home, my thoughts often returned to that session. For the most part, despite good educations, women who graduated earlier than my class did not seek careers but found fulfillment as wives, mothers, and homemakers. Women who graduated some years after my class (Baby Boomers, Gen Xers, Millennials, Generation Z), on the other hand, took their careers and the juggling act of work and family for granted. They were fulfilling a pattern they had observed and planned for.

My generation had a much more complicated and even confused story to tell. When we were in high school, we expected to spend our lives in traditional roles. Sometime after that—in fact, at different times for different reasons—unprecedented numbers of women born during WWII switched tracks and pursued careers. None of us remember thinking, *Well, of course that's what I'll do*. Instead, we opened closed doors and moved in what seemed to be the right direction until the next door appeared, then repeated the process. By trial and error, we became proficient in careers that we never imagined. Combining careers and children presented novel challenges, but we were young and energetic. I assumed we were among the role models that the younger alumnae observed, inspiring them to think, *Well, of course that's what I'll do*.

I wanted to determine how well this model held up across my generation of war babies. What I found was a story of women that begged to be told, though not in the way that I originally envisioned. When I started work on the book, I saw myself as a social psychologist writing a research-based nonfiction account of a generation of women. By the time I completed the interviews of women across America, I had become a memoirist, helping a generation of women tell their stories in a collective memoir.

Along the way I found a coauthor (a longtime colleague, Kendra Bonnett), an editor, a publisher, and a terrific book designer. The marketing and merchandising that followed on the heels of the publication of *Rosie's Daughters* (now in its second edition) has been as explosive as the book itself. Through our blog at RosiesDaughters.com and through social networking on Twitter, Facebook,[2] and Pinterest,[3] Kendra and I have connected with thousands of women.

Did I mention merchandising? To make book presentations and book signings livelier, I wanted to wear a red and white polka dot bandana just like Rosie wore. I searched the Internet and couldn't find anything like the authentic one, which had a random pattern of large polka dots.

I thought about making one, but there wasn't even a fabric that would work. So I had a graphic designer create the pattern and commissioned a few silk-screened bandanas. After presentations, people asked, "Where can I get one like that?" and wanted to purchase one like mine, so I sold the extras I had made. The ones I had quickly sold out, and soon I was getting twelve hundred bandanas at a time. Today, I order in batches of three thousand and have fabric dyed exclusively for us. Kendra and I sell thousands of these bandanas every year to women who want to make a statement about their own sense of empowerment. It's a most gratifying connection. We sell our entire product line through Etsy.com.

But *Rosie's Daughters* had legs that went beyond merchandise. Its publication brought me into the larger sphere of memoir writing and its importance as a literary genre.

Telling personal stories is a valuable form of healing for many writers and storytellers. It's also a source of inspiration, encouragement, and insight for readers. Kendra and I launched our blogsite Women'sMemoirs.com in February 2008, and today—more than one thousand posts later—we are connecting with thousands of people each month. This started us on our path of working with memoir writers, both published and aspiring. Now we teach, coach, and consult on writing and book marketing.

And yes, we also developed products for memoirists—teas for writers, Thai silk journals made exclusively for us, mugs with inspirational messages, and more. I took videos of my all-day memoir writing workshops and turned them into a product with twenty-one video lessons; this let us reach a much broader audience than possible when only teaching in person. And the list goes on.

After four years of workshops, online classes, live events, coaching, and speaking about writing, Kendra and I undertook the book that would address many of the problems that we saw our students have. We had developed a new conceptual framework that became *Writing Alchemy: How to Write Fast and Deep*.

Like Rosie the Riveter, authorpreneurs have a "We can do it" attitude. And that's what you need in today's marketplace. Publishing—indeed most industries—are experiencing dramatic change. At first blush the changes appear to cause more chaos than opportunity. But with an open mind, an aggressive can-do attitude, and a willingness to embrace change and make it work, we can more than survive the turmoil; we can make it work to our advantage.

In the case of publishing, with cash advances having all but vanished, with the disappearance and consolidation of many older publishing firms, and with the very real problem of being discovered when traditional bookstores go out of business, we also have many new opportunities—the rise of e-books, social media, and print-on-demand publishing and bookselling juggernauts like Amazon. We have exciting new ways to make our mark.

We have much more flexibility than ever, and by publishing yourself, no one is going to control your product. Put it out there, build your platform, market yourself, create a following. It can take a while to break through, but if you have something readers/customers want, you can generate a following. Or if you decide to go with a small- or mid-sized publisher—actually any publisher—you'll find that the more you bring to the table, the more of an authorpreneur you are, the more successful you will be with the additional assistance of a publisher.

If you have an idea, a dream, a passion, follow it…even if it's never been done before. Be the first.

SUPER AUTHORS

We studied the industry and identified authors who are literary stars in the writing industry. They have put on their super author mask, tights, and cape and they move forward in an uncommon boldness with the bravado of an undaunted courageous word warrior. Ladies and gentlemen, I would like to introduce super authors who are on the rise. They are…" faster than a speeding bullet, more powerful than a locomotive, able to leap tall buildings in a single bound."

THE FAMOUS SAYING THAT IT TAKES A VILLAGE TO RAISE A CHILD HOLDS TRUE WITH WRITING A BOOK.

MARINA CORYAT
THE DUE SEASON PROPHETESS

Marina Angelica Coryat is the Owner of Refined Communications, LLC. She is an innovative, strategic and results-driven business relations leader with extensive experience in public affairs and community relations in corporate, non-profit, and governmental arenas. Marina has a solid track record to lead and inspire by positively creating strategies, developing programs and building strong relationships. Some of her experience has been for organizations such as Blue Cross and Blue Shield of Texas, McDonald's franchise owners, and the City of Houston.

Her expertise was sought by State Representative Senfronia Thompson to be on her staff as her Communications Director. She currently serves in the capacity while overseeing her public relations business and ministry. Marina was also a political candidate on the November 2019 ballot for Houston's City Council and is considering the 2023 City Council race.

In addition to her work, Marina is a Lifetime Member and Ambassador of the Greater Houston Partnership, the largest chamber of commerce in the Houston area. Her desire is to see individuals grow to their fullest potential and reach their destiny. This drives her passion for having served as an Advisory Board Member for both United Way's Career and Recovery Resources, Inc. the Houston Area Urban League (HAUL). She was also the HAUL Fund Development Chair and was the Co-chair of HAUL's 49th Annual Equal Opportunity Day Gala held June 17, 2017. For several years, Marina was a Mentor for a little boy in the Big Brothers and Big Sisters program.

In 2018, SunArise International Ministries was founded by Minister Marina Coryat in Houston, Texas. This ministry was founded to spread the gospel of Jesus Christ and bring healing. The foundational scripture for this ministry is Malachi 4:2. Marina hosts a weekly broadcast on Facebook Live and YouTube to give a word of encouragement to those who a surviving through the perils of the pandemic and life.

Minister Marina Coryat is a member of the IMPACT Network Global under the leadership of Apostle John Eckhardt who is her Spiritual Father and apostolic covering for SunArise International Ministries. Minister Coryat is a graduate of Kingdom School of Ministry headed by Dr. Cindy Trimm as well as a graduate of the School of the Prophets under the leadership of Apostle Debra Ford and Dr. Linda Calloway of Faith International Ministries who licensed her in ministry on April 23, 2007. Minister Coryat has recently joined Greater Grace Church-Houston and will be supporting the Kingdom of God to advance though this local house. She was an active member of the Windsor Village Church Family for years where she led the 12 noon prayer altar team, served on the Miracles and Healing Team, as well as the Deliverance Team. Additionally, she has served in various ministry capacities at Lakewood Church, Love Ministries Family Church and Shekinah Throne Room Worship Center and St. Benedict Catholic Church.

Marina holds a Bachelor of Arts degree from Cornell University in Itha-ca, New York. She is pursuing her Master of Communication degree from Walden University and her anticipated completion is May 1, 2022. Marina is also a graduate of Leadership Houston, Trimm Institute for Global Leadership, as well as the Center for Houston's Future. She has received numerous awards, including 2016 Top 30 Influential Women in Houston.

In addition to her notable achievements, Marina is the author of her first book, The Due [Dü] Season. Her book is also available in Spanish as La Temporada de Cumplimiento.

EMAILS:
marinacoryat@gmail.com
marinacoryat@refinedcommunications.net

WEBSITES:
www.marinacoryat.com
www.sunarise.org
www.refinedcommunications.net

MARINA'S TIPS FOR ASPIRING AUTHORS

Writing a book is not simply putting letters on a page. It is a written legacy that educates, inspires, and through this can share the story about the author, another individual or place. To that point, there is a lot that is involved in the process. With this being a reflection on the author, an author can want to handle every step of the process. It can be compared to a mother-to-be wanting to make sure everything is ready for her baby to be birthed. The initial thought of writing a book can be exciting, overwhelming and joyous all at the same time.

The first step is to recognize that this is a process. Yes, you may write the book quickly but there is the copyright, the editing, the rewriting, the forward, the cover, another set of editing, and marketing your book. The famous saying that it takes a village to raise a child holds true with writing a book. When you can get help from spiritual mid-wives and aunties and uncles, it can really help.

TIP 1: Get a good support team around you to work on your book, as well as to be there for comfort when the discomforts of pushing out your book baby comes.

TIP 2: Expect the unexpected. Give yourself the time to do this legacy project right.

TIP 3: Pray. Pray for wisdom, favor and direction. According to Luke 2:52 (ESV) where Jesus increased in wisdom and in stature and in favor with God and man, let this be our portion, in Jesus name.

Writing a book is an accomplishment. You will look back and know that you completed something that will remain for years past your life and can extend to places your feet may never have an opportunity to go. Leave your mark in this earth! It's your Due Time!

Marina Angelica Coryat, Author

The Due [Dü] Season

La Temporada de Cumplimiento

WRITING A COOKBOOK IS A CHALLENGING YET EXCITING TASK.

CHEF DIANA RILEY, COOKING ON PURPOSE

Chef Diana Riley is a multifaceted, passionate, and purposeful woman. She is a mother of five. She is passionate about self-love, personal development, growth and prayer. Chef Diana Riley graduated Chef John Folse Culinary Institute at Nicholls State University. Diana is a military veteran where she graduated Top 5 in her military occupational specialty and received an Army Achievement Medal among other awards. She is also the Author of *Cooking on Purpose: Life Lessons Learned from the Kitchen* and *Grace at the Kitchen Table,* she is the host of Kitchen Table Conversations with Chef Diana podcast. She has also co-authored *Resilient Warriors: Stories of the Perseverance of Women in the Military* along with 21 other women veterans in honor of the 22 veterans each day who take their life. She has been a feature author at Essence Fest, and Congressional Black Caucus Foundation for 3 years, and has also been featured in Swagher, VHM, and 225 magazine.

Chef Diana Riley's mission is to serve others through her boutique cooking company and teach the fundamentals of cooking and the significance of sharing simple, nutritious, affordable and pleasing meals with family. She teaches how to cook for educational, self-care and entertainment purposes.

Besides operating a business, she is a Certified ProStart Educator, teaching high school students culinary arts. Diana is a member of the American Culinary Federation and 100 Black Women of Metropolitan Baton Rouge. She is also an avid reader, writer and loves spending time outdoors with her kids, gardening and bike riding. To learn more about Chef Diana Riley and The Kitchen Table, LLC visit www.dianakitchentable.com.

CHEF DIANA'S TIPS FOR ASPIRING COOKBOOK AUTHORS

Writing a cookbook is a challenging yet exciting task. For chefs, you already have many recipes. Recipes you have created and recipes that have been shared along your journey. I will share three tips to help you get started to compile your recipes into a notable cookbook.

1. Do your due diligence as a chef. Research and review your recipes. Recipes should be easy to read and include every component of a recipe. Sometimes you might write a recipe specifically for you to use but when you're gathering recipes for a cookbook it should be formatted for everyone to read.

2. Become a good steward of time. Schedule some time for not only writing but testing your recipes as well. If you have never written a book before, you will need to adjust your schedule to complete the task. Writing a recipe for a cookbook is very different than writing a story. You will also need to schedule time for a test kitchen. I suggest you hire a writing coach preferably with knowledge of cookbook writing.

3. Invest in your self-care. That's right become the best version of you so you can devote time and energy to producing a cookbook. Chefs are trained to work in a challenging and overwhelming environment and working conditions are exhausting. We can become burnout and overlook taking time to recharge in our week after long hours. Go back to step 2 and become a good steward of time and make time for yourself as well.

SHE STRIVES TO PASS A WEALTH OF SELF-REFLECTION AND RESPONSIBILITY TO HER CHILDREN, HER CHILDREN'S CHILDREN, AND HER GREAT-GRANDCHILDREN.

DR. BARBARA WALKER-GREEN, FROM DISSERTATION TO CHANGING THE WORLD FOR WOMEN

Dr. Barbara Walker-Green holds a Doctorate in Business Management and spent her research years studying social and cultural challenges for women across the world. Barbara's dissertation research inspired her to write about social issues and their underlying causes particularly when it comes to women and their struggles in Western society.

Her 20 years of experience as an award-winning financial advisor lends to her ability to identify pain points, reveal them, and be a guide to informed choices. Barbara's debut book, The Inevitable Rise of the Shero Nation, speaks clearly to her skill with identifying pain points, unpacking their origin, and divulging paths for resolutions. This debut book will be followed by a sequence of books relevant to social and cultural discovery and revelation.

A native Californian, Barbara currently lives and works in Sugar Land, Texas. She spends most summers traveling the world and meeting new people. She holds true to her family Inevitable Rise of the Shero Nation 126 motto "3-deep" whereby she strives to pass a wealth of self-reflection and responsibility to her children, her children's children, and her great-grandchildren.

Her legacy is also responsible for passing this motto on until generational wealth is realized, each generation responsible for reaching three generations deep. The wealth of family traditions, self-actualization, financial stability, and service to the community is the wealth to be communicated.

Barbara is a natural educator dedicated to supporting family and those who look to her for advice with the gifts of wisdom and expertise that she has been blessed with. Barbara has been interviewed and quoted by such media giants such as Forbes, Dow Jones, Fox News and RTTNews, has been on the cover of industry magazines, and has been seen on local news stations in the Houston area such as FOX, KHOU, and ABC as a local financial professional.

BARBARA'S TIPS FOR PREPPING YOUR DISSERTATION FOR WRITING A BOOK

1. Have a clear and deliberate focus on the subject matter that you will research for your dissertation subject and do not veer from it throughout your journey.

2. Staying on point with all research papers written during the doctoral process for these papers will give you a strong foundation for your book.

3. Maintain a well-organized library of all of your source materials and keep a well-organized database of your citations.

YOU ARE YOUR BRAND, SO IT IS IMPORTANT TO BE YOUR AUTHENTIC SELF.

AMY M. LE, PUBLISHING DYNAMO

It wasn't until I experienced a knee-dropping life experience that writing became the lifeline I needed to pull me out of despair. It wasn't agoraphobia or anthropophobia, but it might as well have been. When my mother, Snow, the light of my life and the hero of my existence, passed away, I felt lost. The only cure to the void was to write. Not only was it therapeutic but also eye-opening as I unearthed my mother's history and hence discovered my heritage.

I began my writing journey in 2017 and for two years, I lived as a hermit, hiding from the world to wallow in my depression and write my mom's story. Despite receiving a traditional publishing offer, I ended up indie-publishing my debut novel, Snow in Vietnam, a fictionalized biography of my mom's amazing story of survival after the fall of Saigon. Two books followed that one to complete the Snow trilogy in which I shared our family's escape from our home country, our refugee experience in the camps, and our settlement in America.

The moment I wrote my first page, I knew I was never going back to corporate America. I made a conscious, intentional decision to rebrand myself as an author.

AMY'S TIPS FOR ASPIRING AUTHORS

If you want to be a successful author, my first tip for you to become a super author is to develop an author brand. You are your brand, so it is important to be your authentic self. Whatever makes your heartstrings vibrate, that is what you should immerse yourself into. I am a Vietnam War survivor and a Congenital Heart Defect warrior. This means anything having to do with refugees and the CHD community has my full support. When I partner with an organization, when I donate to a cause, when I volunteer and collaborate with someone, I do it with intention knowing I am true to my passions and inspirations. Find your niche because that is where your readers are and if you are presenting yourself as authentic, you'll find your street army of followers who'll support you in anything you do. They will buy your books, write reviews, recommend you to their network, and share your work! You should always be living your brand. What you wear, for example, should represent your work. I have backpacks, stickers, shirts, pens, and all sorts of merchandise that showcase my books or my Quill Hawk Publishing company. Yes, as an indie author, I created a publishing LLC, not only to represent my work but also other authors' works.

Quill Hawk Publishing (QHP) was established in December 2019 to help emerging authors fulfill their dreams of publishing via the indie route. Its mission is to amplify diverse voices. Authors retain their royalties and rights. Quill Hawk Publishing consults to get them to the publication finishing line. For a nominal, one-time fee, authors receive two International Standard Book Numbers (ISBNs) registered with Bowker under the QHP umbrella, bar codes, book cover templates, free IngramSpark title set up codes, help with the book launch, promotional graphics, book reviews, and one-on-one consultation on formatting, uploading, cover design, and more!

Tip number two to becoming a super author is networking. *But I am an introvert*, you say. *I just want to write; I don't want to do any of the public stuff.* Guess what? That's alright if you want to be a writer and sell one hundred copies of your book… but if you want to be read and sell thousands or millions of copies, you have to suck it up, Buttercup, and promote your work. The first step to promoting is networking. Once you've hounded all your friends and family members to buy, read, and review your book(s), you have to network to get more readership. If you're like me, who dream of having her books adapted to film and want to see her stories acted on the big stage or streamed online, you must network. Join Facebook groups and writing communities. Engage with your followers. Seek out organizations where your audience may be. Read a lot of books, blogs, and articles, then participate in panel discussions, forums, conferences, workshops, etc. If there isn't an event that suits you, create one! I wanted to do a panel discussion on preserving history for API Heritage Month and when I couldn't find one, I mobilized one. I also wanted to see local authors come together for a book signing event that also supported a non-profit organization. When I couldn't find one to join, I created one called Books and Bruises!

You can expand your comfort zone by starting small. Challenge yourself to participate in an event once a month. Give yourself a time limit or goal. For example, go to an event for ninety minutes or speak to one person for thirty minutes. Once you achieve the goal, give yourself permission to leave and feel good about it! Rest and recharge for a job well done. Next time, give yourself 120 minutes at an event or sixty minutes with a stranger. Before you know it, you won't recognize the shy, introvert you once were!

People who meet me think I am an extrovert. It is the biggest lie. You see, the more you do this, the bigger your comfort zone becomes. Introverts are the best networkers. We are authentic and we love one-on-one interactions. We love to listen and engage in this way. The more often you do this, the bigger your comfort zone becomes and the more people you intimately know. Suddenly, you walk into a room and you know just about everyone because you've had those deep conversations. Suddenly… the world thinks you're an extrovert. And if you're already an extrovert or ambivert, you're ahead of us!

Alright, so you've created your brand and you're the ultimate networker. What else? My third tip to becoming a super author is to promote. Promote every day. Your inner voice is saying, "I don't like talking about myself. I don't want to come off as conceited or a braggart." I get it. As an Asian woman, I was raised to keep my mouth shut, live in the shadows, be humble and obedient, self-sacrifice for the greater good. Being quiet and living life with one's head down was how my ancestors survived centuries of persecution, war, and colonization. Here's what I have to say about promotion. Start with people you trust and who love you. A small ripple can cause big waves, my friend. One person can be the catalyst for change. Promote your work to your inner circle of trust and ask them to share with their circle of trust. That's the key. Ask. You must give them a call to action. Telling and sharing is one thing but giving your network a task can move mountains!

You must promote every day with intention. Repeat after me. *I will promote every day with intention.* Let's say a friend or family member tells you he loves your book. Get a quote from him and ask permission to post that. Let's say a reader wrote a review on Goodreads, Amazon, BookBub, or wherever. Share that review on social media. Let's say you're writing your next book and your cat is drooling on your keyboard. Yup, share that! Promoting begins now, not after you've published your book. The rule of thumb to promoting on social media today is 80/20. That means 80% of your posts should be an insight into your world as an author such as your research, a reading from your manuscript, your search history, etc., and 20% of your posts should be an insight into your personal life, such as your pets, family, vacation trips, etc. You want your readers to invest in your work, feel like they are a part of your writing journey, relate to you as a person, and be excited when your book publishes.

Promoting also includes marketing and advertising. We are all hustlers, whether it be for our day job, our passion project, our family, or ourselves. Collaborate with people and businesses who support you and your genre of writing. Spend the $5/month on Facebook ads or $300 for that writing conference. Exposure is a good thing. Pitch to an agent or query a publisher. Yeah, it's scary, but we grow and develop by pushing through our fears and experimenting to see what works.

Listen, whether you rip off the bandage in one flinching pull, or you do it slowly, millimeter by millimeter, at the end of the day, the bandage is off. Your journey to becoming a super author can be swift or methodical but you'll get there. Believe in yourself. Lean into your network of supporters. Be a trailblazer, because, Baby, you're already on the path to super authordom.

DON'T LET
YOUR FEAR GET
IN THE WAY OF
YOUR DREAMS.

BETSEY KULAKOWSKI, THE MASTER WEAVER OF FANTASY NOVELS

Betsey Kulakowski is a federally trained investigator and has 30+ years of experience as an occupational safety specialist, with a degree in emergency management. Betsey served on disaster response teams at the Murrah Federal Building Bombing, the World Trade Center, and Hurricanes Katrina/Rita, as well as other disasters in Oklahoma.

She wrote her first book at age 6. Being a writer wasn't something she chose. It chose her.

These days, between working on the next book in the Veritas Codex series, she runs a small nonprofit organization and enjoys camping, hiking in the mountains, and drinking coffee by the water. She also enjoys cooking and considers red beans and rice over a campfire her signature dish.

She's married and has two grown children, and a spoiled Boston Terrier.

The Veritas Codex is her first published novel, followed by The Jaguar Queen (Book 2), The Alien Accord (Book 3), and The Monk's Grimoire (Book 4), which was released March 1, 2022. There are more books to come in the series.

Visit her website at www.authorbetseykulakowski.com

BETSEY'S TIPS FOR ASPIRING WRITERS

1. Don't let your fear get in the way of your dreams. Being a writer takes courage but sometimes the only thing in your way is you. Move over.

2. Write every day. Whether it's five words of 5,000 words. Do what you can with the time you have.

3. Don't quit! You never know how close you are to achieving your goals. You got this!

READERS LOVE BOOKS THAT ALLOW THEM TO PEEK BEHIND THE CURTAIN, TO LEARN THE SECRETS OF AN UNFAMILIAR WORLD (LIKE THE JUSTICE SYSTEM). LET THEM FEEL THAT YOU'RE GIVING THEM THE INSIDE TRACK.

WILLIAM BERNHARDT, THE MASTER OF LEGAL THRILLERS

William Bernhardt is the author of over fifty books, most recently the Kenzi Rivera legal thriller series, starting with the #1 bestselling novel *Splitsville*, and the six Daniel Pike novels, starting with the #1 bestselling novel *The Last Chance Lawyer*. His previous works include the Ben Kincaid series, the historical novels *Challengers of the Dust* and *Nemesis*, two books of poetry (*The White Bird and The Ocean's Edge*), and the Red Sneaker books on fiction writing. In addition, Bernhardt founded the Red Sneaker Writers Center to mentor aspiring writers. The Center hosts an annual writers conference (WriterCon) and small-group writing retreat. More than three dozen of Bernhardt's students have subsequently published with major houses. He is also the president/owner of Bernhardt Books, which publishes fiction, poetry, and creative nonfiction under several imprints.

Bernhardt has received the Southern Writers Guild's Gold Medal Award, the Royden B. Davis Distinguished Author Award (University of Pennsylvania) and the H. Louise Cobb Distinguished Author Award (Oklahoma State), which is given "in recognition of an outstanding body of work that has profoundly influenced the way in which we understand ourselves and American society at large." He has been nominated for the Oklahoma Book Award nineteen times in three different categories, and has won the award twice. In 2019, he received the Arrell Gibson Lifetime Achievement Award from the Oklahoma Center for the Book.

In addition to his novels and poetry, Bernhardt has written plays, a musical (book and score), humor, children stories, biography, and puzzles. He has edited two anthologies (*Legal Briefs and Natural Suspect*) as fundraisers for The Nature Conservancy and the Children's Legal Defense Fund. In his spare time, he has enjoyed surfing, digging for dinosaurs, trekking through the Himalayas, paragliding, scuba diving, caving, zip-lining over the canopy of the Costa Rican rain forest, and jumping out of an airplane at 10,000 feet. In 2013, he became a *Jeopardy!* champion.

OSU has called Bernhardt "Oklahoma's Renaissance Man." In 2017, when Bernhardt delivered the keynote address at the San Francisco Writers Conference, chairman Michael Larsen noted that in addition to penning novels, Bernhardt can "write a sonnet, play a sonata, plant a garden, try a lawsuit, teach a class, cook a gourmet meal, beat you at Scrabble, and work the *New York Times* crossword in under five minutes."

WILLIAM'S TIPS FOR ASPIRING WRITERS

1. Prepare. Organize your thoughts in a structured outline. This will stimulate your creativity, not restrain it.

2. Readers love books that allow them to peek behind the curtain, to learn the secrets of an unfamiliar world (like the justice system). Let them feel that you're giving them the inside track.

3. Revise and revise and then revise some more. Readability is everything in popular fiction. Refire your prose until every single sentence is immediately clear.

SEEK THE ENDORSEMENT OF ESTABLISHED PROFESSIONALS OR EXPERTS TO BUILD YOUR AUTHOR PLATFORM.

RHONDA JENKINS, THE DELAY IS NOT DENIAL EXPERT

Rhonda is a 21st Century woman of faith who balances work and family. She often shares her personal testimony from meager beginnings to her rise as one powerful voice in the infertility space. Her multifaceted career experiences as professional counselor, entrepreneur, mentor and motivational speaker has prompted thousands of women around the country women to candidly dialogue about their reproductive health.

During her journey to motherhood, Rhonda recognized the limited resources for women who are experiencing infertility, loss or delayed parenting. She felt compelled to break the silence and provide hope to generations after successfully enduring a nine year journey of her own. This desire to help other women led to the creation of Sparkles of Life, Inc. in 2008. This non-profit organization provides a variety of programs for women in all stages of conception and delivery, including the Garden of Life IVF Grant.

Rhonda host education forums to support women who have struggled with infertility, miscarriages, delayed parenting and surrogacy.

Sparkles' dynamic work has been endorsed as "Life Changing Support" by International Ministers Forum. She has received the "Pillar of Strength" award from the National Women of Achievement, "Pioneer" award from League of Business and Professional Women and served as a Goodwill Ambassador in Houston for the Freedom Foundation of Victoria Island, Lagos, Nigeria.

Rhonda's highly anticipated book, released in May 2014 is packed with pearls of infertility wisdom and inspiration. With contributing author, Dr. George Ndukwe, "Delay is NOT Denial! - A Victorious Journey to becoming a Mom" will continue to inspire individuals for years to come. Rhonda received a Bachelor of Arts degree from Le Tourneau University.

RHONDA'S TIPS FOR ASPIRING AUTHORS

1. Don't be afraid to tell your story.

2. Seek the professional help of an author's assistant.

3. Seek the endorsement of established professionals or experts to build your author platform.

CONNECT WITH SOMEONE THAT CAN HELP BRING THE STORY OUT OF YOU AND GIVE YOU STRUCTURE AND A PLAN.

DYLAN RAYMOND, MILITARY TRANSITIONALIST AND AUTHOR

Dylan Raymond also known as the Military to Civilian transition expert. He is bilingual and fluent in Military and corporate speak. Dylan is a dynamic speaker, passionate coach, mentor, and consultant. His passion is serving the Military & family members.

Dylan was recently highlighted in the Stars and Stripes and on LinkedIn as an influencer and military advocate to follow. He is the author of Rucksack to Briefcase a Military to Civilian transition guide for servicemembers and their families and Amazon bestselling book titled Put Me in Coach, Vol 1. Dylan holds a Bachelor's degree in Business Administration from University of Maryland, University College.

Dylan has a distinguished 25+ year Army career which includes 2 overseas combat deployments. He held two of the most challenging roles in the Army, a Drill Sergeant, and Field Recruiter in NYC during 9/11.

DYLAN'S TIPS FOR ASPIRING VETERAN AUTHORS

1. What should I write about? Everyone has a story or a solution, so it's that one thing that bothers you the most or even stretch you to where you are challenged and afraid…that is probably your starting point and key topic.

2. Connect with someone that can help bring the story out of you and give you structure and a plan.

3. Start writing (don't worry about structure right now) leave a journal to write in, by your bed, in the car, record your thoughts on your phone and transcribe later…. just write!

READ
CLASSICS.
THE OLD
STUFF.

PAMALA J. VINCENT, THE BADASS AUTHORPRENEUR

Born into a military family, Pam spent her formative years in North Chicago before moving to Hawaii and enjoyed her jr. high and high school years there. In ninth grade she met a handsome surfer. They married two months following college graduation and recently celebrated 45 years of married life (51 together).

Pam Vincent is a 38-year veteran teacher who just recently retired her alternative jr. high and high school TREC Academy (Taking Responsibility for Educational Choices). TREC closed in 2015 to allow her time to care for an ailing relative. She began writing at an early age to express her feelings and moved from amateur to professional author in 1994. Closing the school in 2015, allowed her to enter the fulltime writing market.

As a gymnast (back in the dark ages), Pam quickly learned training was expensive and entrepreneurship was in her blood. When she was told she was too old to train for the Junior Olympics, she developed her first level of "Watch me!" She won a 4th place medal two years later.

To put herself through college she waited tables at a local restaurant and worked as a national gymnastic judge.

After receiving her degree, she spent ten years teaching kindergarten and coaching competitive gymnastics for Clackamas Community College. Two babies joined the family and the Vincent's home settled into daily life. It was not long after the second baby's arrival that an injury occurred ending Pam's coaching career. She took a job as the principal of a Christian school. That lasted until the babies were old enough to go to school, and mom and dad took on the job of homeschooling. As her oldest reached jr. high age, other jr. high families in the community asked if she would school their children too. Although many told her it couldn't be done, her "watch me" spirit surged again and TREC Academy was born.

TREC was an alternative school for jr. high and high school students. Often the students were sent to her by the principals of local schools when a student was either falling behind, or so advanced that they were bored. Pam was appreciated by undercover police officers, gang task force officers, and US Marshals, because their children often became targets in public schools. She also mentored and tutored night school for ex-gang members returning for GED's or Diplomas. Her love of teaching to the students' needs with uniquely created curriculum won her the Teacher of the Year Award for Alternative Schools in Oregon four years running.

TREC was filled to capacity for 21 years until God closed the doors to move her on.

So, what's she doing now?

She is a faith-based, family friendly screenwriter, non-fiction inspirational author, writing mentor and business coach. She thrives on equipping the underdogs of the world to successfully reach their goals and dreams. She shares her step-by-step "watch me" strategies to get them from here to there on their journey.

Pam has written twenty-one books, her latest, *Dare to be a Badass*, won the Non-Fiction Writer's Association Silver Award. Her website, Dare to Be a Badass, equips women to find their voice, their power, and their purpose. She also teaches individuals how to start home-based businesses. Many of her clients build their platform with a book to open the door for speaking engagements and further opportunities. Their dreams develop from concept, to chapter, to publication and marketing their precious messages. She also teaches and can create clients' websites to broaden a client's their social media presence.

The value of the Dare to Be a Badass organization is:

- Lifehacks for surviving everyday life without sacrificing confidence.
- Tried and tested personal and professional coaching either in a one-on-one setting or in a large group of like-minded warriors.
- Get featured on our S'Hero page and promote your business.
- Professional strategies to make you relevant in today's market.
- A cheerleader for the underdog and those who think they can't 'do it'
- We may start out as coach/client, but we end up as friends!

Pam is passionate about families, and particularly supporting women (and single dads) as they fight to hold families together spiritually, and financially while keeping their sanity. She believes there is gold in each person and strives to bring that unique quality to warrior status. Because she has seen the battle firsthand, she is a strong advocate and cheerleader.

She writes for *Huffington Post, Ten to Twenty Parenting, Addicted 2 Success, She Owns It, The GoodMen Project, Inspire, Wisdom Pills,* and several other online magazines. Pam is a featured guest on several podcasts as well as her own two weekly podcasts. Two of her articles have gone viral—by learning the vital social marketing game!

She is the creator, editor and writer for Dare To Be a Badass and Between a Rock and a Teenager, both are practical tools offering opportunities to learn how to cast off all that encumbers our flight and to soar!

When she is not writing, you will find her in the garden with her trusted black lab by her side, drinking a white chocolate mocha with dirt under her nails!

PAM'S BEST TIPS FOR ASPIRING WRITERS

1. Read classics. The old stuff. There's a rhythm and dance learning to line up words to strike chords in a reader's heart. The classics have staying power because they've done it right. Study them. Dance with them. They'll help to develop your own vocabulary and dance.

2. Stay in your lane. If you're a fiction writer, write fiction. If you're a non-fiction writer, study the craft. Find those who are doing it well and analyze what they do. Even the great artists started out imitating the masters until they found their own style. It will help you build your platform. If you try to be something to everyone, you won't know who your audience is.

3. Use the tools available to you –Grammarly, dictionaries, thesaurus, topic studies, industry standard rule books (Strunk & White). These tools will keep you from looking like an amateur even when you are one.

4. Grow a thick skin but seek advice. Find a mentor who will take you under their wing and will show the ropes, give you critiques to move you forward. Let go of your book babies and let others edit/critique and give you the good, bad, and ugly feedback. Lick your wounds, know why you're writing and for who, and move on. It's the only way to get better. When I look back on my first writings, I was so proud of, I'm embarrassed, but I was out there doing it! You can too.

5. Learn to do what only you can do and delegate the rest. Invest in the tools for your writing career.

6. Writing is neither glamorous nor immediately lucrative. It takes hours of hard work. Be willing to put in the butt in seat hours to hone your craft. Set writing goals and celebrate the wins.

7. Believe in you! Develop a "watch me" attitude and then go at it!

IMPROVING YOUR CRAFT WITH EACH BOOK IS IMPORTANT.

KEVIN WAYNE JOHNSON, EXCELLENCE IN MINISTRY EXPERT

Because, he says, "God uses ordinary people to accomplish extraordinary things," Kevin Wayne Johnson has taken up the task of developing individual and organizational operating excellence as his life's ministry. He trains, mentors and coaches in order to coax audiences to live out their gifts, and in the words of his national best-selling book series, to then "Give God the Glory!" This series of eight books has earned the current radio and former television co-host some 19 literary awards, since 2001. Gayle King, an editor-at-large for O, The Oprah Magazine, praised his work, writing to him that "Your book, Kevin, touched me."

Johnson is the Founder & CEO of The Johnson Leadership Group, LLC, and an independent certified coach, trainer, mentor and speaker with the internationally recognized John Maxwell Team, where he leads learning experiences that are tailored to meet the specific needs of the audience to help maximize efficiency, growth, awareness and effectiveness. He provides organizations, and the people who work within them, with the tools to forge effective personal and interpersonal communication and delivers training on the elements of dynamic relationships, to equip teams with the attitudes and attributes needed to develop individuals into leaders. He does so through motivating workshops, seminars, insightful keynote speeches and compassionate coaching – all to encourage personal and professional growth.

Johnson enjoyed a 34-year career (retired) in government and private industry as a frontline, mid-level and senior -level leader. He led workforce development, training, organizational change, acquisition/procurement, customer service, client relationships, budget, security, records management, property administration, facilities and human resources organizations during his tenure. He was a key leader on the National Performance Review for Procurement and Customer Service Reform, under the first Clinton Administration, has testified before the

U.S. House of Representatives Small Business Committee on Procurement Reform and wrote testimony that was presented before the District of Columbia's Committee for Government Operations.

A native of Richmond, Virginia, Johnson earned a B.S. in Business Administration and Management from Virginia Commonwealth University's School of Business and completed course work towards an M.B.A. at both Marymount University and the University of Colorado at Colorado Springs. He earned the Master's Certification in Government Contracting from The George Washington University, Washington, DC. He is an ordained Church of God Ministries, Inc. (Anderson, IN) minister and has served in a myriad of leadership positions over the past 21 years in the local church, to include Senior Pastor, as well as regionally, nationally and internationally in Kenya Africa, St. Lucia, Turks and Caicos, and London England. His latest book – Leadership with a Servant's Heart – is an Amazon.com best-seller in two categories and earned 9 literary awards in 2020 and 2021. Johnson is currently serving a 4-year team as Faith Community Commissioner for Suicide Prevention under Maryland Governor Larry Hogan.

He lives in Clarksville, Maryland with his wife of 29 years, Gail, and raised three sons. He has one God daughter and two Grand God daughters.

KEVIN'S TIPS FOR ASPIRING AUTHORS

1. Use active social media posts to "groups" as well as recurring posts thanking family and friends for the support.

2. Building relationships with bookstore managers and owners in your local area as well as nationally with chains like B&N to partner on book events that draw in book buyers.

3. Improving your craft with each book is important. Your writing should get better and better and meet the needs of the book buyers - both retail and consumer.

WRITE THE BOOK, IT WILL BE HERE FOREVER.

JAZMIN AVE' ANDERSON, MEDIA MOGUL AND MARKETING DYNAMO

Jazmin Ave' Anderson is an American Radio/Television Personality, Accomplished Author, and Media Entrepreneur—on a mission to connect people across the globe. She has spent over 10 years hosting events as well as radio and television shows from coast to coast.

Today, through radio, TV, podcasting and social media, Jazmin is connecting people with every aspect in their life spectrum…be it mentally, physically, emotionally, economically, socially or spiritually with the objective to add relevance and positive contributions to their lives.

Jazmin is the President of JTV ONE Global Television where she writes, produces, and interviews prominent quests from the entertainment, business, and health industries, getting them to share their stories on how they became successful as well as how they have overcome their obstacles.

Through her in-depth interviews and other communication venues, she strives to encourage and uplift people through everything she does professionally and personally.

Jazmin has built her journalistic portfolio by interviewing celebrities, musicians, athletes, etc. And one of her main questions has always been about their journey to living a RICH life. She has taken the valuable nuggets from her interviews and those she gathered from her personal journey, to give you a success that shares her ten prevailing thoughts on RICH living. Her Ten Golden Rules for Living a Rich Life was published in August 2017, in her first book entitled "Live Fully." Jazmin is the author of 3 books in total. "Live Fully Journal" and "A Powerful Woman."

She is a beautiful person-both inside and out, with an ambition to intentionally share her influence for good through the world of diverse media connections, and her personal contributions to society.

JAZMIN'S TIPS FOR ASPIRING WRITERS

1. Write the book, it will be here forever.

2. Always market your book, tell new people about it daily. Be a vendor at events and conferences.

3. Come up with a challenge for each potential reader and record them sharing their perspective based on your title and what it means to them. Use that clip to help promote your book.

AUTHORS ARE TRULY SUPERHEROES BECAUSE THEY "DARE TO GO WHERE NO MAN HAS GONE BEFORE," AND WRITE THEIR WAY INTO THE HEARTS AND MINDS OF THEIR UNSUSPECTING AUDIENCE WITHOUT SPEAKING A SINGLE WORD.

CLOSING THOUGHTS

Authors Are Superheroes!!!

It was my mission to introduce you to fifteen sensational individuals who have mastered authorship, in hopes that you could find some similarity to you, your mission, or vision for your book writing career. Space wouldn't allow me to share the story of every author I have the privilege of knowing, but hopefully you will walk away from this reading experience knowing more than when you started.

It takes a lot of courage to be an author. Especially in the 21st Century when the new literary pathway to success is still being charted. I liken being an author to being a hero. The other day I happened to being looking for synonyms for the word "heroes" and the following words were suggested: Supermen (women), Champions, Conquerors, Idols, Brave Men (Women), Stars, and Leads. Now all of these words speak of individuals who perform above and beyond their human ability. It is my opinion that authors fit in every last one of those categories. Here's why:

- Authors are supermen and superwomen because they can lift unusually large boxes of books and a pop-up stand with a single hand while talking to their agent on their cellphone in the other hand.

- Authors are champions because they still meet publishing deadlines while suffering from acute writer's block.

- Authors are conquerors because they often persevere against the odds of getting their book published and survive the hundreds of rejection letters that they receive when pitching a new manuscript.

- Authors are idols that humbly receive the praises of their loyal readership.

- Authors are brave men and women who work hard to balance their work/life schedule with their writing schedule.

- Authors are stars because they light up a room with their intellectual brilliance.

- Authors uphold the lead because they are trailblazers, dreamers, and innovators creating new paradigm shifts in the thinking and emotional responses of their readers.

- Authors are truly superheroes because they "dare to go where no man has gone before," and write their way into the hearts and minds of their unsuspecting audience without speaking a single word. Now that's powerful!

To all my fellow superheroes,

Happy Writing

Sharon

ABOUT THE COMPILER

Sharon C. Jenkins

"Authorpreneurs are a rare breed. They authentically combine two skill sets, writing, and entrepreneurship, to create a space in the literary marketplace for their creativity." **Sharon C. Jenkins**

Sharon C. Jenkins is the Inspirational Principal for The Master Communicator's Writing Services. Her business provides writing and coaching services to small businesses, nonprofits, and authors. Known as The Master Communicator, she has mastered multiple forms of media communications in both writing and speaking. Her professional experience ranges from working as an editor for a major, minority-owned communications and marketing company to being a senior publishing consultant for an award-winning publishing house.

She is a best-selling and award-winning author. Her expertise includes business communications, entrepreneurship, book coaching, publishing, and marketing. She is affectionately known as a "literary midwife" and has helped hundreds of authors "birth" their book babies.

Her solo projects are comprised of the following titles: Beyond the Closet Door, Christ's Rescue from Abuse, Authorpreneurship: The Business Start-Up Manual for Authors, and The Super Author Journal, and a host of e-books tailored for authors on such topics as writing, marketing, time management, and publishing. Her most recent print release for authors is a compilation titled, Are you a Super Author? This book has the "How to Get It Done" stories of 14 seasoned authorpreneurs loaded with tips from their journey. It was intentionally designed to be a literary inspiration for the aspiring author interested in starting a business in writing. Sharon's most recent e-book release is Maximize Your Book Sales with Data Analysis written with award-winning author Mike Kowis. She started her journey as a poet, graduated to a playwright, and is now an award-winning, Amazon bestselling author, blogger, and podcaster.

Sharon has been a featured blogger on Huffington Post, The Good Men

Project, Self-Published Author, Afrovibesradio.com, and Book Marketing Tools. She also hosts her radio show Luminance on Houston-based Galaxy Gospel Radio. Sharon is also a board member of the award-winning Brilliant Women in Film, who directed and produced her mini-documentary, The Birthing of a Book Baby. She has been the conference host for multiple writers' conferences, the latest event was the Write Your Book in 90 Days, in conjunction with The Living Your Dreams Conference in the scenic West Virginia Mountains at Alpine Lake Resort. She has also been a featured panelist or speaker at national, regional, and local events such as WriterCon, the Authors Marketing Guild, Houston's Writefest, Living Your Dreams Conference, 2019 Marketplace Fair's Author Showcase, Houston Independent Authors' Writers Lunch, Nonfiction Authors Association, and the Houston Writers Guild. For more information about Sharon go to www.supersuthorgranny.com.

INTRODUCING ...
SUPER AUTHOR GRANNY

She's a walking reference and resource book on all things that relate to super authors and publishing. For more information go to www.superauthorgranny or check her out on a social media platform near you!

www.ingramcontent.com/pod-product-compliance
Lightning Source LLC
Chambersburg PA
CBHW071115030426
42336CB00013BA/2091